Coach

by Toshi Naito

Harcourt

Orlando   Boston   Dallas   Chicago   San Diego

Visit *The Learning Site!*

www.harcourtschool.com

The soccer players stand on the sidelines. They are watching their team play and everyone is excited.

The score is 4 to 4. The two teams are tied. They have made the same number of goals.

One of the teams tries to make a goal again. The players cannot get the ball into the net.

The game is almost finished. The coach yells, "Time out!" He says, "Stop the game for a little while!" The coach tells the players to meet on the sidelines. Everyone thinks about the game. How can they win?

The team needs a coach to help them win. Usually a coach makes a plan and draws a diagram, or picture of what the team needs to do. The coach and the players review the new plan.

The coach may tell the players to guard the other players. The coach may tell the players to set up the goal.

This will be hard!

"You can do it!" says the coach. A coach always encourages the players. Now the team has a good plan. The players run back on the field.

The team plays hard. They guard players. Some players run along the sides. They kick the ball hard, and the ball goes into the net! The team makes a goal! They score! The coach's plan worked!

The team is happy. The coach is very happy. Everyone is ready to make another goal. Run up the sides, guard the players, kick hard! The ball goes into the net, and the team scores again!

Now the score is 6 to 4.

Time is up! The game is over. The winning team is very happy. Everyone jumps up and down because they are excited. The coach is proud of the team.

"You did it!" says the coach.

All sports have coaches. Coaches know
almost everything about a game or sport.
Players need coaches to play the game well.
Coaches know what their players can do.
Coaches help their teams do their best.

A baseball team has many coaches.

Some coaches show how to bat. They can help players hit the ball better. A coach can show a player how to catch, too.

Some coaches show how to pitch. They can help players throw the ball better.

Some coaches stand at the bases. They tell the players when to run and when to hit the ball.

Usually a coach stays near the bench, as a player takes the bat and tries to hit the ball.

Strike one! The player does not hit the ball.

Strike two! The player misses the ball again!

The player tries again, and cannot hit the ball. "Strike three! You're out!" The player goes to the bench.

A coach tells the team, "Work hard. Have courage. Do not be afraid. You know what to do. You can do it!"

Football has many coaches, too.

There are throwing coaches. A throwing coach shows the players the best way to throw a ball. They help players get stronger and throw the ball faster.

There are running coaches. A running coach shows players how to run faster.

There are kicking coaches. A kicking coach helps players kick better. Players learn how to kick the ball to the right place.

There are tackling coaches. They show players how to stop the other team from making a touchdown.

During a football game, the coaches stand at the side of the field. They tell the team when to play. They tell the team when to come in.

The coaches tell the team how to play, and the team listens to the coaches.

The players run fast. They tackle the other players. They throw the ball carefully. They want to score points.

The coach tells the team, "Work hard. Have courage. Do not be afraid. You know what to do. You can do it!"

Not every sport is played by a team. Divers can be part of a team. They also can dive alone.

There are diving coaches. They help divers learn to jump and twist.

Divers need courage. They cannot be afraid. They dive into the water from high places. They do flips and twists. People cheer and clap.

Coaches help divers do better. Coaches help divers learn new ways to move. Coaches tell divers, "Work hard. Have courage. You know what to do. You can do it!"

Basketball is another sport. It is played by a team. The team works together to score points.

Basketball coaches help players learn to move and jump. The coaches teach players how to bounce the ball and run at the same time.

The players move very quickly. They run back and forth. They bounce and throw the basketball.

The coaches stand at the side. The coaches tell the players what to do.

During a basketball game, the players pass the ball. They throw the ball into the basket to score. Swoosh! The ball goes into the basket!

When the players score, the people cheer and clap. People stomp and shout. Basketball is a very noisy game!

Coaches help the team work together. They say, "Work hard. Have courage. Do not be afraid. You know what to do. You can do it!"

What sport do you want to play?

Maybe a coach will help you play the sport better. Coaches are special people. They care about the players and want team to do their best.